ECHOES OF A LOVE THAT NEVER WAS

PREETHIKA

For those who loved deeply,
lost painfully,
and learned that some goodbyes never truly end.

Contents

Foreword

Love is often painted as a fairytale—one that always finds its way to a happy ending. Some love stories are not meant to last forever. Some are meant to teach us, to change us, to shape the way we see the world and ourselves.

This book is a journey through love and loss, through hope and heartbreak. It is a story of two souls who found each other, held on with all their might, and yet, had to let go. It is about the kind of love that lingers—one that refuses to be forgotten, even when life demands otherwise.

Preface

This book is a journey of love, longing, and the bittersweet reality of letting go. It is about two people who found a home in each other, only to realize that love alone was not enough to keep them together.

As I pen these words, I am not just recounting a story—I am retracing footsteps, reliving remnants of laughter, broken promises, and the silence that lingered in their wake. This is a story of love—real, raw, and beautifully flawed. A love that endured time, distance, and the weight of fate's unyielding hands.

This book is also an effort to acknowledge that sometimes, our hearts romanticize friendships and weave fantasies of love. The ripple carried forth leads us to lose 'what is' in the pursuit of 'what could be'.

In the story, there are moments when we believed love could conquer everything, and there are moments when the fact that it could not pierced our hearts. Through it all, we hold on, sometimes with hope, sometimes with fear, and sometimes with the stubborn refusal to let go.

Because sometimes, love, no matter how fleeting, never truly fades.

With all my heart,
Preethika

Acknowledgements

This book is a piece of my heart, woven with memories, emotions, and the love that once was. It would not have been possible without the presence of certain people in my life, who shaped this journey in ways they may never fully realize.

To my home, for being the inspiration behind these words. For the love, the friendship, and the lessons that came with it. Our story may not have had the ending we once dreamed of, but it will always be a chapter I cherish.

To my family, for their unwavering support, even when I struggled to put my emotions into words. Your love has been my anchor, my safe place.

To my friends, who stood by me in silence, knowing when to listen and when to remind me to heal. Your presence made the hardest days a little lighter.

To every reader who has ever loved, lost, and found themselves in the spaces inbetween, may you find comfort in knowing that love, even when it does not last forever, is never wasted.

With gratitude and love,

Prologue

Amid the chaos of life and the unpredictability of relationships, there are always stories that weave into friendship, love, and self-discovery. This is one such story, of two souls whose paths crossed in the most unexpected of ways despite having countless ways to meet before, fate chose the most unexpected moment to bring them together but it planted the seeds of a bond that would grow and evolve in ways neither could have anticipated.

From the innocence of strangers, to friendship, to the intense emotions of love, and heartbreak, P and J's journey is a testament to the enduring nature of true companionship. Through the highs and lows, the laughter and tears, they discovered not just each other, but also themselves. The book chronicles their intertwined paths, capturing the essence of their relationship through a series of chapters- healing , growth, understanding, acceptance, and ultimately finding peace in the realisation that some people are meant to be friends, even when love does not turn out as expected. The story is not just about love, but about the beautiful complexity of human relationships and the enduring power of friendship.

Characters

J, A person who embodies the qualities of a true lover and dreamer. Handsome and charismatic, he has natural charm that draws people to him, yet he remains discerning about those he lets into his life. For those he values, he is unwaveringly loving and dedicated, willing to put in the effort to nurture and sustain meaningful relationships. J is not just romantic, he is a man driven by dreams and ambitions in life. His love for his family is profound, and he harbors and works hard to make their lives better and to make them feel proud. Works to turn his dreams into reality. J is such a walking green flag or could even say existing green forest and anyone living around him definitely living in a green universe. For any girl, J represents an ideal partner. His blend of passion, ambition and understanding makes him someone many would dream of being with.

P, a brown-eyed girl, curly hair, her skin like milk chocolate- she's a sight to behold under the sun. Apart from the physical traits that make her desirable, she's blessed with a heart of gold; which hates rarely, forgives quickly, and loves deeply. Though life has robbed her of her innocence quite early, she does not bear a negative filter when going through life. She values people even though they once meant harm to her. One might call it foolishness, but it is a strength in this world gone bad. She never disregards another person's feelings, but makes them feel seen and wanted. She has strong convictions but is not egoistic to admit her faults. She is stubborn but not on a destructive level. She has an eye for aesthetics and is responsible in all that she is entrusted with, be it work,

people, or love.
If she's a colour, she would be white, cause she accepts everything without judgement, you can always find a piece of you in her. And if she's a feeling, she would be love. Cause she embodies all its tenets to almost perfection. She's the kind of person who will stick by you when the whole world walks away. Her thoughts could seem plain one moment, but there'll be times when they teem with meaning and profound intention. She's the loudest laugh you'll hear in the room, but the quietest scream. She is a mystery when she chooses to be - even if storms are raging inside her, you wouldn't have a clue until she lets you in.
She's always got love on her mind. Even though life's handed her the short hand in that aspect, she still believes in it - a fairytale love.
In the face of true love, she is an unstoppable force because she truly believes that "all is fair in love"!

CHAPTER ONE

WHEN PATHS COLLIDE

It was October 14, 2021, a day like any other, yet destined to be anything but ordinary. My friend Lyn and I were out with our group, enjoying a carefree afternoon. As our time with friends drew to a close, Lyn mentioned she wanted to meet someone special. To her, he was more than a friend but not quite a lover; to him, she was something more than love. She asked if I would join her, and I agreed, not knowing this encounter would change everything.

We stood at a busy junction near Orchid Square, a spot where the road leads towards Dolphin Nose. As Lyn called him, she gave me a quick rundown about him. "He's a Mallu." she said, though she could not recall exactly where in Kerala he was from. In no time, a sleek, black, polished Verna pulled up, gleaming under the afternoon sun. It reminded me of the way Arabs in Oman maintained their cars—immaculate and pristine.

He was wearing a black sweatshirt and shorts, paired with dark blue Crocs. His car, clearly new, still wrapped in seat covers, crinkling with every movement. The attention to detail in his car's upkeep impressed me, hinting at his meticulous nature.

Lyn introduced us, "Preethika, this is Juno, and Ju, this is Preethika." she said. Juno, exuding a palpable confidence, barely glanced my way and replied with a curt, "Okay." without making eye contact. His dismissiveness struck me. He seemed fiercely loyal to her, and his aloof attitude triggered a spark of defiance in me. I matched his attitude, deciding not to engage further.

We went for a drive, with Lyn and Juno immersed in their own world. I observed quietly, noting the nuances of his behavior and their interaction. The drive was smooth, the conversation between them flowing easily, while I remained an outsider in this bubble they had created. Eventually, Juno dropped us back, and the encounter ended as unceremoniously as it began.

Yet, that brief meeting lingered in my mind. Despite his aloofness, or perhaps because of it, Juno had made an impression. It was an unexpected beginning, one that hinted at the complex journey that lay ahead for the both of us.

CHAPTER TWO

BEYOND WHERE THE EYES MET

At first, I never thought I'd want to know Juno better. His attitude had put me off during our initial meeting, and I dismissed him as someone not worth the effort. But as fate would have it, we found ourselves constantly thrown together. It was always Lyn, Juno, and me, navigating the ebb and flow of our intertwined social lives.

As time went on, Lyn began to confide in me about the ups and downs of her relationship with Juno. The more she shared, the more I realized that he deserved so much more than what he was getting. I was taken aback by the lengths he would go for her—the little things he did and the unwavering support he offered. It was surprising, almost astonishing, to witness how deeply he cared for her, and it made me think that a guy could love with such intensity and devotion. Secretly, I began to wish for a guy like him, not knowing that he would eventually become mine.

I became the quiet anchor to his storms, a solace woven into his restless tides, trying to help him see the reality of his situation. I gently encouraged him not to expect too much from Lyn, as she seemed incapable of giving him the commitment he deserved. This became my routine—putting sense into his head, even though he rarely seemed to realize the truth. Despite this, my heart softened toward him. It pained me to see him not receiving the love he so freely gave, and I decided that, even if he couldn't reciprocate it, I would give him the love he deserved.

In my quest to know him better, I discovered the little details that made him who he was. I learned about Miya, his beloved cat, his favorite snack—orange Lay's chips, and his preferred drink, Mountain Dew. We began texting every day, sharing the events of our lives, our thoughts, and our feelings. With each message, my appreciation for him grew. I valued him deeply from the very beginning, and as our conversations deepened, I knew that my feelings were justified.

Juno's capacity to give love without expecting anything in return was both heartbreaking and inspiring. He was a rare soul, one who deserved to be cherished and loved fully. And so, I made it my mission to be the person who would give him the love he deserved, hoping that one day, he might see me not just as a friend, but as someone who truly cared for him.

CHAPTER THREE

MIRRORED WOUNDS

This was, without a doubt, the most heartbreaking phase of Juno's life. It wasn ot just his struggle—it became mine too, in ways I had not anticipated. He was caught in a cruel tug-of-war between what he wanted and what was never going to be. He yearned for something more than friendship with her, but she did not want that. She refused to set clear boundaries, leaving him stuck in a painful void, always hoping, always waiting. It broke him in ways I could not bear to witness.

Juno clung to the belief that if he kept trying, kept giving, something might change. He convinced himself that one day, she would love him back. But everyone around him, including me, could see the truth. It was not going to happen. I knew her just as well as I knew him, and every moment of denial on his part made the truth weigh heavier on my heart.

As time passed, his hope turned into desperation, and his desperation began to destroy him. He was unraveling, losing himself bit by bit, and it was agonizing to watch. I tried to reach him, to make him see what he was doing to himself. I begged him to stop chasing something that was hurting him more with each passing day. But my words were just whispers in the storm of his emotions. He couldn't hear me—because he was in love. And love, I learned, can make even the strongest people blind.

The worst moment came like a knife to my soul—27 cuts, each one deeper than the last, etched into his skin in a desperate attempt to release the pain he felt inside. I will never forget the sight of his hand, blood oozing out like a silent cry for help. My heart shrank at that moment, overwhelmed with an ache so profound it felt like it might consume me.

I didn't tell him how I felt back then. I didn't have the words for the emotions that churned inside me—anger, sorrow, frustration, and love, all tangled together. All I could think was that he was crazy. Crazy for loving someone who could not love him back. Crazy for not seeing how worthy he is. Crazy for thinking his pain was his alone, when every drop of his blood felt like it was draining from my heart too.

It was not just her that drove him to this point; there were other battles waging inside his mind. The healing process was not just about healing the wounds on his hand— it was about stitching up the ache in our hearts. I hoped it was also soothing the invisible scars on his soul. And silently, I prayed that he would one day see himself through my eyes—a man worthy of love, but not like this. Never like this.

CHAPTER FOUR

Unsettling Silence

When I moved to Bangalore, I did not think much would change between Juno and me. We had our routine. I would text him every day, sharing little things about my new life in the city. It was comforting, like a thread tying me to a piece of home. But what I did not see coming was how quickly everything would change.

The last time we spoke was September 9, 2022. I did not know it would be our final conversation, but something shifted after that. The texts stopped. He stopped.

Then, on October 4, my phone lit up with his name. A missed call. My heart raced at the sight of it. I could not hide the happiness I felt. Something made me feel right all over again. But just four minutes later, a message followed, stealing that joy away. "Called by mistake. Tried to add another friend." That sting was sharper than I cared to accept. I replied with a simple "Ok." though my mind was swimming with questions. Why had he stopped talking to me? Why did this hurt so much?

Weeks passed, but the silence lingered. My thoughts became a restless loop of questions and doubts. On

November 4, I broke down and sent him a message: "Are you pissed with me for something, Juno?" No reply. The silence was deafening. Two weeks later, on November 20, I sent another desperate "??"—but still, nothing.

By now, I had started telling myself that maybe this was how things were meant to be. Maybe we were just two paths that had crossed and now parted. But even as I told myself to let go, my heart refused to listen. I could not help but think that this was about her. She never liked me putting sense into his head, never liked how I was always there for him. And Juno, ever the hopeless lover, would not dare upset her, even if it meant hurting himself or me. December came, and with it, the weight of the year gone by. On December 26, I sat down to write him a message—not to send, but to save. It was a habit of mine to thank the people who mattered most at the end of every year, and no matter how things had turned out, Juno was still that person. I poured my feelings into the note, telling him how grateful I was to have met him and how much he had meant to me.

And then, as if the universe had been waiting for the right moment, my phone buzzed. His name flashed on my screen. My heart stopped. A message. Then another. My hands trembled as I unlocked my phone, barely believing what I was seeing.

"It's crazy for me to come and text you now, I know."

My heart raced as I read his words. He apologized not just for the silence, but for everything. He did not explain why he had pulled away, nor did he want me to ask. "Don't ask me why or what I did," he wrote. I could not stop the smile spreading across my face. My chest felt lighter, as though a weight I did not even realized I was carrying was lifted. It was as if a bird that had been caged for far too long was suddenly set free, its wings aching to soar.

But the part that stayed with me, the words that settled deep into my soul, was when he said: "I've put an end to going back to her." That was all I wanted for him all along. Not for me, but for him to realize his own worth. His message was not just an apology, it was an acknowledgment of his value. He had chosen himself finally. At that moment, I felt complete. His healing felt like my own. And as we picked up the threads of our connection, I realized that sometimes, even the deepest silences have their purpose.

CHAPTER FIVE

A NEW DAWN

Juno had finally broken free from the tangled mess that was his "situationship" with her. It was not even a proper relationship, but the pain it caused him was very real. When he decided to move away from her, she did not seem to care. Perhaps she knew deep down that she had messed things up beyond repair. He confided in me, and my heart felt heavy once again. His emotional rollercoaster became mine, and I struggled to accept the hurt he had endured because of her.

He revealed that he had been in Bangalore for a while, hoping to spend time with her before leaving for the UK. What made it worse was that he lied to his parents, telling them he was working in Bangalore. Now, with no reason to stay, he faced the daunting task of going back home. How would he explain everything to his parents? The question was thrown at him.

To make ends meet, he resorted to working for Rapido as a bike taxi driver. It was a soul-crushing experience. For every 100 rupees he earned, a significant portion went to the app's commission, leaving him with almost nothing. His friend Nissan did his best to support him, but it was a difficult time.

One day, Juno called and asked if I could join him to Commercial Street. He wanted to buy some gifts for his mom and younger sister before heading home. We went shopping, picking out a pair of footwear for his mom that I chose and a few hair clips and other cute girly stuff for his sister. There was an awkward silence between us, but we both tried to break it by talking about anything and everything. He opened up about his struggles and the details of what had happened with her. Listening to him, my eyes welled up with tears. It hurt to hear about the hardships he faced because I knew he deserved so much better.

After shopping, we headed back to S.G. Palya to grab a bite. On the way, every bump in the road made me hesitate to hold onto his shoulder for support, unsure of how close I should get. We found a small cafe and ordered pasta and our favorite musk melon shake. We ended up having five of them, trying to savor the moment.

He dropped me back at my PG afterward, leaving me with a whirlwind of thoughts. There was something between us, something unspoken that I did not want to complicate. But our connection had revived. The silence that once separated us began to dissolve, making way for a new beginning. His ending with her marked the start of something beautiful between us, a connection forged in shared pain and newfound hope.

CHAPTER SIX

Hues Within the Shadows

After Juno let go of the weight that had been crushing his spirit, it felt as though life offered us a chance to rewrite our stories - a blank page. While he wrestled with his demons, I was enduring a storm of my own, one that shattered me into countless fragments. It was not love that broke me; it was something deeper, darker, and entirely my own. He had no idea about my struggles; they unfolded silently in the shadows during a time when our paths had drifted apart.

One night, the phone rang, and I heard the raw ache in his voice. He broke down, his tears spilling through the line, flooding the silence with his pain. It was his breaking point. I tried to piece together his shattered words, soothing him as best I could. He told me that it helped, but even his reassurances could not quiet the worry gnawing at my heart. His mental health became my priority. Checking on him became as instinctual as breathing. If he was not okay, I felt compelled to pull him back from the edge.

Then, one sleepless night, the roles reversed. In a moment of vulnerability, lulled by exhaustion, and the comfort of his voice, I let my guard slip. My pain, buried deep during our separation, spilled out like a river breaking its banks. But I did not linger on it; my focus was still on him. Yet, in that moment, we became two broken souls, finding refuge in each other's scars. Without realizing it, as I helped him gather his strength, I began to rebuild myself. His healing mirrored mine in a way that felt both accidental and fated.

Our nightly calls became a sanctuary, a lifeline tethering us to each other. Gradually, the weight lifted from his shoulders. He began to laugh again, and each small spark of joy from him reignited something within me. As we grew closer, an unexpected longing awakened in me—a desire to do something extraordinary, something that no one else would dare to do. I wanted to show him how deeply he mattered, how uniquely he had touched my life.

I sifted through countless ideas, dismissing each one as too ordinary. Then, like a whispered revelation, the idea of a tattoo emerged. A permanent mark, etched on my skin, symbolizing us. But it could not be just any design; it had to capture the essence of our bond. After hours of contemplation, I knew what it had to be—a house with a plant growing through it, cracking the roof yet breathing life into the walls.

Why a house? Because he always called me home. To him, I was the place where he could rest, where he felt safe. And the plant? It was us—a testament to resilience, to how we grew despite the cracks, how we turned brokenness into beauty.

When the tattoo was complete, I could not wait to show him. I video-called him, teasing him with the promise of a surprise. He tried to guess, but when I finally revealed it, his reaction floored me. His eyes shimmered with tears, his face alight with a smile I had not seen in far too long. That smile—radiant, unguarded—was worth every ounce of pain I endured. His cheeks flushed, and in that moment, the world felt still.

That act, so simple yet profound, drew us even closer. It was a silent vow, etched in ink and sealed in tears.

Soon after, I introduced him to my family. Juno was not just a part of my life anymore—he was a part of me. My soul stitched to his' in ways words could barely capture. My family embraced him warmly and he slipped into our lives as if he was always been meant to be there. Our time together, surrounded by laughter and love, became a reservoir of memories we would draw upon for years to come.

Through him, I rediscovered something I thought was lost forever- a sense of belonging, a quiet peace that whispered, you are safe now. Healing him had mended the broken pieces of myself, and in that shared journey, our bond grew unshakable.

We were no longer just friends. We were two souls bound by the delicate threads of pain and healing, creating a love so profound it felt like poetry—a love that turned scars into art and made even the darkest nights feel like home.

CHAPTER SEVEN

MARKED BY THE MOMENT

Months passed, and we grew closer and closer, but everything was through calls and texts. Something was missing—the tangible touch of love. We yearned to meet each other. The urge to see each other intensified every day as our love deepened. He was in Coonoor, and I was in Bangalore. He could not come to Bangalore because his parents suspected something had gone wrong the last time he was here. The only way we could meet was if I went there, but I did not have any holidays. I wished time would fly so I could see him and feel the warmth of his embrace. Onam arrived, and though I usually went home for the festival, this year I stayed back in Bangalore. I regretted it deeply because Junaid was home—not his house, but mine. He was invited over to my house. He called me and asked if he should go, and I told him, "Why not?" even though he said it would not feel the same without me.

He went, sending me snaps of him drinking with my dad, chilling with my brother, and enjoying my mom's home-cooked sadhya. How lucky was he? On the other hand, I was crying during my classes. At one point, I stopped crying and decided to go home. I called my brother right away, asking him to book my tickets and told him not to inform my parents or Junaid because I wanted to surprise them.

I left that night and halfway through my journey, I told Junaid I was coming. But fate was unkind to me, as always. Junaid had to return to Kerala that same day and he would not be coming back as he would leave to the UK directly from there. Yes, this was going to be our last meeting. The last.

As soon as I reached Coonoor, I went home to surprise my mom and dad, dropped my luggage, brushed, and changed my clothes. Even before the sun rose brightly, Junaid came home to pick me up. His car was parked beside our house compound. My heart beat like someone was trying to save a life. As I walked towards him, I could see him through the windshield, though the glare obscured him a bit. He had his phone in hand, facing the passenger door. I opened the door, but not completely, as it would hit the wall. Half-opened, I stood there, holding my phone, fidgeting nervously. I had never felt this nervous before. It was a new feeling. The first thing I asked him was, "How did you know I was going to wear black?" He simply answered, "I know you, Preethi." We both wore black, coincidentally. We kept looking at each other. I asked him if he was showing off his new watch or phone case because he had his right hand next to the steering wheel, holding his phone towards me. He said, "Why can't you still see it?" I asked, "See what, Junaid?" I looked around and saw a bunch of red roses, thick silver bangles, oxidized jhumkas, and silver nail polish. My heart stopped. No one had ever done this for me in my entire 19 years. It was at that moment that I knew what it felt like to be special. I don't remember saying anything. I was stuck, needing time to process and cherish the moment. Junaid was taking a video, which was why he had his phone with him. I thought my surprise would be the highlight of the day, but Junaid's surprise overshadowed mine. I always told him that I liked red roses, so much that even when I die, he would have to bring me those. He knew I was addicted to jhumkas and the nail polish- I randomly mentioned that I saw a girl wearing silver nail polish in college, and I liked it. He noted all of this and bought them for me, just to see a smile on my face.

I got into the car—last time, it was a scooter; this time, it was a car. Last time, I didn't know if I could hold him from behind, and this time, I didn't know if I could put my hand over his while he was changing the gear. He asked me to promise that we would not talk about this being our last day, and I sadly promised. We went for a drive, stopping at a spot where we had gone before with a few others. We parked the car on the footpath, walked into the green tea estate, and followed a narrow stone path leading to a huge rock. From there, we could see so many things, the whole of Kotagiri, just as I saw so many emotions in his eyes. We sat down, the weather chilly and sunny. Silence surrounded us. We talked about random things, then our eyes met. We got closer, our lips touched, and until that moment, I couldn't believe we were going to kiss. His eyes were closed, and so were mine. I could feel his breath on my face, our fingers in each other's hair, then my hand on his face, like ice on a flame. It was not a long kiss, but the memory would last forever. Once he kissed me, his first kiss, I knew it would never be the same again. My heart skipped a beat, caught in the moment. He pressed me to his heart, and my world fell apart. It was as if he cast a magic spell on me, as if heaven was sighing. It felt like two souls promising, "I am yours and you are mine." We didn't talk about it, but I knew we both wanted to kiss again, this time longer, but we knew it wasn't the right place. We clicked a few pictures. My favorite was the one where he was kissing me. His dad kept calling him because he had to leave. We walked slowly towards the car, holding hands. We got in. The windows were up, the car facing the main road. We looked into each other's eyes and kissed again, this time longer. I kissed him with my eyes open because I wanted to see how he felt. For a few minutes, I kissed him with fear, fear that someone would see us. Later, the thought of this being our last day made me kiss him the way I wanted. His phone rang—it was Ippa. He ignored it and continued kissing. Ippa called again. It was a sign that we had to stop, or we never would. We laughed. He had to go collect something from a place instead of his dad. We got his work done and went to my house. Before we got out, we kissed again. A white car came in front of us and honked. It was my brother. Junaid pushed me away, saying, "Shit, it's your brother." I was calm since my family kind of knew. My brother always gave me space. Junaid wasn't feeling okay. He stood where my brother's car was parked to see if my brother could have seen us. I told Junaid not to worry. He came inside my house with me to say a final goodbye to my parents. Nothing struck me; I was still lost in thoughts of our first kiss. My brother, Junaid, and I walked towards the gate. Junaid and I hugged. He wanted to kiss me but couldn't because my brother was there, so he gave me a forehead kiss. That was when I realized he was leaving and this was our last meet. I didn't know when I would see him next. A year later? Two? No idea. He got into the car, and when he turned the key, it hurt me. He moved the car slowly, then stopped. He got out and walked towards me with his black T-shirt that smelled like him and his perfume. That broke my heart. He handed it to me without saying anything because my brother was there. His look said it all. He left, and through his right mirror, he looked at me, waving and bidding goodbye. My heart trembled. I ran to the terrace to watch him leave. He was gone, leaving me behind with untold love.

CHAPTER EIGHT

HELD BY THE HORIZON

September 3rd, 2023—the day I dreaded with every fiber of my being. It was the day Juno was leaving for the UK, and we would be 4,166 miles apart. The distance loomed like an insurmountable chasm, threatening to swallow our love. It wasn't just hard; it was heart-wrenching to watch him go, knowing I wanted more time, more moments, more of him. Yet, he had to leave to build his career, and I couldn't stand in the way of his dreams.

In the days leading up to his departure, I found solace only in solitude. I would retreat to the washroom to cry, the walls bearing silent witness to my grief. I clung to our photos, knowing they would soon be all I had to remember the moments we shared. My emotions were a storm, but I tried to shield him from the worst of it. After all, for me, it was about letting him go, but for him, it was about leaving everything—his family, his home, and me.

Unable to voice my feelings directly, I sent him video messages, my face tear-streaked, my voice trembling. The thought of not knowing when we would meet again gnawed at my heart. Fear consumed me: Would he forget me?

Would he find time for me in his new life? The different time zones felt like cruel barriers. It was as if my soul was being torn from my body.

Juno, even amidst his own struggles to prepare for this new chapter, never left me alone. He tried, time and again, to comfort me. Every time I called, I would ask, "Juno, will you forget me? What will I do if you forget me, Juno?" And he would reassure me, "No, thangoo, I won't. Let me go figure things out." The only hope I clung to was our love, the bond that had grown between us.

Our journey was set to be one of endless separation and tumultuous emotions. Yet, love knows no bounds. Despite the heartache, I believed that our love would endure, that it would bridge the miles and the time zones. The only solace I had was in our mutual commitment, the hope that our efforts and our love would carry us through.

As he left, I felt a piece of myself go with him. The emptiness was overwhelming, the pain almost unbearable. Yet, amidst the sorrow, there was a glimmer of hope. Our love, tested by distance and time, would either falter or grow stronger. And in the depths of my heart, I believed it would prevail.

CHAPTER NINE

FROM THIS MOMENT ON

It was the 23rd of September, 2023. Junaid was in the UK, and it was around 7 PM in India. We were on our usual call, but there was something different about him that night. His smile was tender, almost secretive, and it tugged at my heartstrings. As we talked about our day, I babbled on about college, but I could sense his restlessness.

He was lying on the sofa, shifting positions, clearly trying to tell me something but holding back. My curiosity mixed with a growing sense of fear. What if he wanted to stop talking? My mind raced, overthinking every possibility.

Junaid sat up, unable to relax. He murmured something, asking me to guess, but my mind was too scattered. Finally, he took a deep breath, his eyes locking onto mine, piercing right into my soul.

"Preethi, can you be my...?" He paused, and in that moment, my heart stopped. Goosebumps prickled my skin, tears welled up in my eyes, and a smile spread across my face. I was in shock. "Be your what?" I managed to ask.

With full confidence, he looked at me and said, "Can you be my girlfriend?"

In that instant, it felt like my entire world bloomed. The happiness that surged through me was beyond words. I felt like I had won the most precious prize in life, something I had been praying for. For the first time, I had won in love. It was the beginning of a new chapter, one I had longed for with all my heart.

We cherished that moment together and I kept asking him how long he had been wanting to ask me. He confessed that he had been thinking about it even before our last meeting in Coonoor. He was hesitant then, unsure if it was the right decision. He revealed that he had talked to Abi, his friend, about whether a long-distance relationship could work. But Junaid was ready. He was ready to face the challenges, ready to fall in love from afar, ready for everything that came with it.

He also told me that he had wanted to do this in person when he would visit me again. He wanted to make it even more memorable, but he realized that waiting would make it too late. It might not have seemed like much effort because we were already deeply in love, just waiting to confess it. Making it official was his way of sealing what we both already felt.

The next morning, I woke up as his girlfriend. I wore his black T-shirt that he had given me, put on his perfume, feeling his presence with me. Because I was his, officially. I posted a story on my private account, with the song "Him & I" by Halsey playing in the background. It felt like I was dressing up to announce to the world that he was mine and I was his. That moment, that simple yet profound confession, had changed everything. It was a memory I would cherish forever, a reminder of the love that had blossomed between us despite the distance. As I lay there, wrapped in his scent and his love, I knew that this was just the beginning of a beautiful journey together.

24

CHAPTER TEN

WHERE HEARTS STILL MEET

I always believed that long-distance relationships were doomed to fail. I thought the distance would be too much to handle, but with Juno, everything was different. It was easier than it sounded, as if the miles between us didn't matter at all. We were determined not to let the distance affect our love.

Juno had his struggles. Finding a part-time job in the UK was tough, and he missed home terribly. He missed his Imma, and was overwhelmed with homesickness. Despite all this, we stayed connected. We were on call almost all the time, living through our honeymoon phase like any other couple. It felt as if he was there with me, sharing my room and my life.

Gradually, our calls extended into the night. Juno would put me to sleep, his voice a comforting presence in the darkness. There wasn't a single night I went to bed without him on the other end of the line. I grew so accustomed to it that I couldn't sleep if he wasn't there. My routine revolved around his. My day became night, and my night became day, all in sync with his schedule. We watched movies together, shared our thoughts on Bigg Boss, and did everything possible to bridge the gap between us. We ensured that neither of us felt alone or overwhelmed by the distance.

I discovered that I was the type of girl who loved keeping my partner informed about every detail of my day. I would text Juno about everything—leaving for college, arriving at college, what I ate, where I went, who I was with, even the weather. Not because he asked, but because I wanted him to be a part of my life in every way possible.

When Juno finally found a part-time job, our routines changed again. Though we had less time together, we made sure nothing caused misunderstandings. He would leave for work at 11 PM India time, and we would be on call until he reached his workplace. I stayed awake until 2 AM so he could call me during his break. We seized every minute we could to be together. His routine relied on mine, and mine on his. Our understanding was deep, and our love grew stronger despite the distance.

The spark between us was undeniable, but it was the depth of our love that truly stood out. Every month on the 23rd, we celebrated our relationship, trying to make it as special as possible. Our protectiveness for each other grew, but it was always in a loving way. Juno even made his friend Nissan deliver things to me when I felt low. Once, when I was on my period, Nissan brought me fries and a tissue with a note on it from Juno. Juno put all his efforts into being the perfect boyfriend.

What kept our relationship strong during the long distance was trust. Juno and I trusted each other completely. We never hid anything because we were always on call. Trust was the key factor that held us together. We had our share of fights, but they were always over small things and never too serious. We never went to bed with a fight unresolved. We made sure to clear the air before the day ended, fighting with so much love.

As the honeymoon phase began to fade, we braced ourselves for the next phase of being in love. The distance made our love grow deeper, and we faced the challenges together, hand in hand. Through it all, Juno was always there for me, and I tried my best to be there for him. Our love story was a testament to the power of trust, understanding, and unwavering commitment.

CHAPTER ELEVEN

A Shift in the Stars

Good days passed, but slowly, the shadows of uncertainty began to eclipse our happiness. The question of our future loomed large in our minds. Could we really be together? Neither of us could be certain. He was a Muslim, and I was a Christian. My parents would likely resist initially, but deep down, I knew they would accept him if he was the one I truly wanted. From his side, however, the answer was a resounding no. His parents weren't open to such things, and we knew it.

Arguments and misunderstandings became more frequent. Our conversations grew colder as our differing perspectives clashed. It wasn't toxic, but the looming uncertainty of our future cast a shadow over us. Despite this, the love and bond we shared never faded. We held on to each other, knowing how deeply we cared. Yet, the unspoken fears gnawed at us silently.

Our love felt like the infinity symbol—one point where the lines meet, representing us holding on to each other, while the rest of the symbol represented the endless loop of silent thoughts about our future. The loop seemed never-ending, just like our unspoken fears.

We didn't talk about how this phase affected us individually. I craved assurance about our future, while he grappled with the uncertainty, torn between fighting for us and going against his parent's wishes. His silence grew more frequent, creating a barrier between us. We stopped expressing our feelings as much, letting fear settle where love once was.

It was a never-ending cycle. We held on to each other, but the silent thoughts about our future weighed heavily. One day, he decided to address the elephant in the room. He told me he couldn't promise anything about our future. He didn't give me assurance, nor did he deny the possibility. But I had faith—not just in us, but also in God. I believed our paths had crossed for a reason.

I tried to convince myself and him with thoughts like, "Why did God let us meet? Why did it take so long for us to find each other, even though I lived close to his house? There were so many chances, but we didn't meet until now." Deep down, we both believed it would end well. Every day at 11:11, we manifested our hopes and dreams, holding on to the faith that love would find a way.

But something was pulling us apart. We didn't want to do this, but we had to. We had to stop texting. It felt like a mini-breakup, a silent one. It was hard, like a sign from God that the world was ending. Everything turned dark. My wishes and urge to be with him burned in my head. Our hands went apart, but our pinkys still clung together.

Days and weeks passed, though our thoughts always found a way to eachother, the reality was a distorted maze. I was lost like a star that fell from the sky lying on the ground, longing for the vast blue that I once belonged to. The unwelcome moment finally arrived, like a dagger to my heart. We broke up, and the blue sky just became a blackhole that swallowed me whole.

CHAPTER TWELVE

CLUTCHING THE LAST STRAND

Weeks went by, and it was draining—draining us both. It felt like someone had bleached the leaves of our relationship, rendering them fragile and transparent. We thought that drifting apart might help us move on, but it only amplied the longing we had. Barely a week passed, and we found our way back. Even though the circumstances grew dim, our urge to stay in each other's lives flamed the dying embers of our relationship.

During this time, my father fell ill, and I was emotionally devastated. The only person who stood by me through that harrowing journey was him. He was my rock and his unwavering support was a beacon in those darkest hours.

Despite it all, the silence grew. It wrapped around us, thick and suffocating. Our conversations shifted. We began acknowledging the possibility that things might not work out. He shared his fears, and I tried to convince him that if we both had the will, we could overcome any obstacle. However, reality had other plans. Our conversations became strained, more like preludes to parting than dialogues of hope. He kept saying he couldn't disappoint his parents, and I couldn't argue against that. I didn't want him to choose me over his family.

He couldn't give me assurance because he feared failing to keep his promise. His love for me clashed with the reality of his obligations, creating a storm within him. It haunted him, preventing him from being himself and speaking openly with me. He was terrified of hurting me. Our talks turned into debates, then arguments. Yet, through it all, the sense of love remained. We were just lost—lost in the relentless question of our future.

It was as if we were on a ship, sailing through a fog that never lifted. Each word, each glance was laden with the weight of unspoken fears and dreams deferred. The silence wasn't just an absence of sound; it was the resounding presence of all our doubts and insecurities. And though we held on to each other, we were drifting apart, like two stars pulled by the gravity of their own destinies.

In the end, it wasn't a lack of love that threatened us. It was the fear of the unknown, the reality that love alone might not be enough. But even as the fog thickened and the silence deepened, there was a part of me that clung to the belief that our love could transcend the boundaries of religion, family, and fear.

CHAPTER THIRTEEN

DARKEST GOODBYE

April had always been my favorite month. My mum's birthday, my own—it was a time filled with cherished memories. But that year was different. That year, my heart was breaking. Juno and I hadn't talked properly for a while, and our conversations had taken a somber turn, leaning more towards letting go than holding on.

April 8, 2024, was the last night we were on call. It was around 1 AM in India. I stood in the dimly lit corridor, my roommate sleeping peacefully inside, oblivious to the storm raging in my heart. I leaned against the rough, poky wall, trying desperately to convince him that we could make it work. My voice trembled as I desperately poured out my hopes and dreams, but his responses were firm and unyielding. "It's not okay for us to do this," he said, "This isn't happening."

His words shattered me. Tears streamed down my face as I wept, standing alone on the staircase. The reality of our situation hit me like a crashing wave—this time, it was really ending. We were actually going apart. I wasn't his anymore, and he wasn't mine. The thought of losing him tore my heart to pieces, along with the dreams we had built together.

I called him "Junu ikka," as I always did, seeking some comfort in the familiar term of endearment. But his response was like a dagger to my soul. "Don't call me that," he said. "I'm not your Junu ikka anymore."

With those words, I slid down the wall, my legs giving way beneath me. My phone slipped from my hand and clattered to the floor. I couldn't speak, I couldn't breathe. I was shivering, my body wracked with sobs. Reality hit me hard—he was really gone. Then I picked up the phone and ended the call, whispering, "It's fine. I'll let you go if you don't want this."

I cried and cried until my body was exhausted, until a deep breath finally came, one that allowed me to accept the harsh reality. That how much ever I could want it, it wasn't happening. Even with all my strength and conviction, I couldn't force it to happen. The dreams we once had were now just fragments of a dreadful reality that were thrust upon me leaving me with no choice but to carry them for a lifetime.

April, once a month of joy and celebration, had become the cruelest month. The rough wall against my back, the cold floor beneath me, the silence of the night—all bore witness to the end of our love story. The night was over, and with it, a part of my heart was gone forever.

CHAPTER FOURTEEN

MOURNING CLOSURE

It was all over, yet something in me still clung to hope. As my birthday approached, I held on to the belief that he would reach out. The week leading up to it was agonizing. Each day felt interminable, time seemingly at a standstill while my heart bled from fresh wounds. And then, as if my silent prayers were answered, he did text me on my birthday. His message was formal, but it still brightened my day. I couldn't unlove him, nor move on, nor hate him. His reasons were valid and both of us were powerless against them. All I could do was understand and accept.

When he confided in me that the confusion in his mind—whether what we had was true love or mere attachment tormented him, that just laid the last stone on my grave. But I couldn't blame him. I might have loved him more than I had imagined, because even though I was utterly broken, not once did a bitter thought take root in my heart.

After April, I texted him on his birthday in June, and we had a brief conversation. Months passed, and in August, something about him resurfaced in my mind. It was a strange feeling, one I had whenever something was wrong with him. I texted his friend, who reassured me that he was okay. That calmed me, but on August 30th, as I was lost in my thoughts, I heard that familiar notification sound, the one I had set only for him. My heart raced, hands trembling, as I opened his message. He had sent me a 7-minute 43-second voice recording, explaining what had stopped him from continuing our relationship. It was a closure.

His voice broke in the recording, and hearing it broke my heart. I felt numb, unsure how to process it all. It was new and painful. I still hadn't moved on. I missed him terribly—his presence, his calls, the way he called me Preethi. I missed sharing every detail of my life with him. I had become so dependent on him for expressing my emotions—love, sorrow, anger. He handled me with the care and tenderness one would show to a fragile flower. But now, where would I go? He was my world.

I had distanced myself from so many people, not that I had many to begin with. I wasn't someone who needed others to make myself okay; I preferred dealing with things on my own. But the no-contact period taught me a lot. Moving on wasn't just about letting go of the past; it was about releasing the future we had envisioned together. It wasn't easy to let go of a thousand memories. I knew it would take at least another lifetime, maybe even more, to let it all fade away.

For me, moving on felt like accepting my fate, but loving him was my destiny. It was terrifying to accept that I would never be able to unlove him, that I would never be able to forget. Forgetting was never an option. A part of me always hoped he would come back. A part of me still believed that things could be set right. I knew a piece of my heart would always belong to him.

In the silent corners of my mind, I replayed our moments together, clinging to the echoes of his laughter, the warmth of his embrace. The love we shared was like an unending melody, a tune that played softly in the background of my life. Every star in the night sky seemed to spell his name, and every whisper of the wind carried his voice.

He was my moon, my guiding light in the darkest nights. And even though our paths had diverged, I found solace in the memories we created. I wore my love for him like a hidden scar, a testament to a bond that was both beautiful and painful. The thought of losing him shattered me, but the love we shared gave me strength.

I would walk through life carrying the essence of him within me, like a secret treasure. Each step I took, each breath I inhaled, was a silent homage to the love that once was and the love that still lingers. For in the tapestry of my heart, his thread was woven deeply, intricately, and forever.

And so, I moved forward, not with the hope of forgetting, but with the hope of remembering. For loving him was not just a chapter in my life—it was the very essence of my being, a symphony that would play on, no matter the silence that enveloped us.

CHAPTER FIFTEEN

WHERE THE SEA MEETS THE SKY

After the closure he gave me, we both knew that we could still be friends, but we also knew that our love was still raw and fresh. If we ever started talking as friends again, we would undoubtedly fall in love once more and find it impossible to move on. So, we chose not to talk as we used to, though we kept checking on each other from time to time. It was awkward, an unspoken agreement to avoid discussing the depths of our feelings.

Perhaps we were meant to be friends and nothing more. Maybe it was us who romanticized our friendship and complicated things. We turned the simple beauty of our bond into something more complex, mistaking our closeness for love. Maybe it was just attachment, and we misinterpreted it, losing what we were truly meant to be in the process.

Our friendship was a sanctuary, a quiet harbor in the storm of life. We shared secrets in whispered conversations and found comfort in each other's presence. We laughed and cried together, creating a mosaic of moments that shimmered with an unspoken understanding. But in our yearning for something more, we wove threads of desire into the fabric of our bond, distorting its pure simplicity.

We romanticized late-night talks, seeing them as declarations of love rather than the sweet communion of souls. We mistook the warmth of companionship for the burning fire of passion, and in doing so, we lost sight of the beautiful friendship that was our true destiny. We were two souls who found solace in each other, but our hearts, in their desire for more, complicated the gentle dance of our bond.

Maybe we were never meant to be lovers. Maybe our true destiny was to remain as friends, forever etched in each other's hearts. We might have lost the love we once imagined, but the essence of our friendship remains.

In our story, we found love in friendship, and in doing so, we blurred the lines between the two. We turned the sanctuary of our bond into a battlefield of emotions, complicating what was meant to be simple and pure. Our journey together was a testament to the delicate balance between love and friendship, and the painful beauty that arises when the lines between them are crossed.

We might have lost the love we once had, but the memories we created will always be a part of us. We will carry the essence of our bond. For now, I will move forward, cherishing the moments we shared, and finding solace in the knowledge that sometimes love is meant to be eternal, even if it exists only in the echoes of our hearts. Our love story may have ended, but the impact it had on my life will remain forever.

In the fabric of life, we were threads that intertwined for a brief, beautiful moment. And while we may no longer walk the same path, our souls will always be connected by the memories of a love that once was and the friendship that will always prevail.

www.ingramcontent.com/pod-product-compliance
Lightning Source LLC
Chambersburg PA
CBHW031512150726
47990CB00007B/2987